A Child's First Pet

Suzanne Lieurance

T.F.H. Publications, Inc.
One TFH Plaza
Third and Union Avenues
Neptune City, NJ 07753

This book has been published with the intent to provide accurate and authoritative information in regard to the subject matter within. While every precaution has been taken in preparation of this book, the publisher and author assume no responsibility for errors or omissions. Neither is any liability assumed for damages resulting from the use of the information herein.

ISBN 0-7938-3111-3

Printed and bound in the United States of America

Printed and Distributed by T.F.H. Publications, Inc.
Neptune City, NJ

Contents

Things to Consider 5

Chinchillas 11

Ferrets 17

Gerbils 25

Guinea Pigs 31

Hamsters 37

Mice and Rats 43

Rabbits 49

Sugar Gliders 59

Index 64

Things to Consider

There are many good reasons for a child to own a pet. According to the American Academy of Pediatrics, "Children who own pets have higher self-esteem, improved social skills, and are actually more popular with their peers." They also learn to accept responsibility and develop a higher regard for all living creatures. But before you rush out and purchase any old pet for your child, it's wise to consider a few things so that you will fully understand the commitment you will be making by bringing an animal into your home.

First, do you have time to care for the pet properly? Very young children aren't ready for the day-to-day responsibilities of caring for a living creature. Certainly, your child can help care for his or her pet, but ultimately, the responsibility for the animal's well-being will be up to you, the parent.

Do you have money for all the things a new pet will need—food, vet check-ups, toys, accessories, and a cage or other enclosure? Generally, the smaller the pet, the less the expense, but even the smallest of creatures will require food, a home, and other materials that can add up to quite a bit of money each year. These expenses should be added to the family budget.

Are you allowed to have pets in your home? If you're renting, check out your lease carefully before you purchase an animal of any kind.

Do you have enough space for the pet when it reaches its adult size? Most small mammals don't require a lot of space, but you won't want to confine your child's new pet to a dark corner of the basement or your child's bedroom, because most of these animals thrive when they're at the heart of the household.

Is anyone in your family (including you) allergic to any particular animal? If you aren't sure, try visiting pet stores with your family before you purchase a pet and see if anyone starts to cough, sneeze, or sniffle.

One important consideration before you buy a new pet is whether you can afford the cage, equipment, bedding, and food your pet will require.

The age of your child is a very important consideration. Very young children must be carefully supervised as they interact with their pets.

How old is your child? Very young children usually do best with a pet that requires a minimum of care and doesn't tend to bite or nip. Do you have time to teach your child how to interact appropriately with a pet? Toddlers (and even older children) must be taught how to approach, touch, and play with a pet, and their time with the animal should always be supervised.

Are there any legal restrictions in your area regarding the type of pet you wish to purchase? The laws concerning the keeping of small mammals as pets are very complex and vary from area to area, so it's up to you to find out the legal status of any pet you wish to purchase. To do this, it's usually best to check with your local Department of Wildlife, Department of Agriculture, Department of Natural Resources, or other governmental body that is responsible for implementing the laws related to species that may be kept as pets in your area.

You should also understand

Veterinary examinations are important to the health of many small mammals, and these expenses should be factored into your family's budget.

that while all small mammals don't require exactly the same care, there are some common aspects to the care of each of these creatures. All of the small mammals described in this book live in a confined space, so you will need to make sure the animal you choose for your child has a comfortable and roomy cage or other enclosure. Animals that are forced to live in spaces that are overcrowded or too small suffer unnecessary stress, which many times leads to poor health.

Each of these small animals needs company. For most (with the exception of hamsters) that means that two or more of the same species should be purchased so that they can keep each other company when members of your family are not around.

Each of these pets needs room and time outside of its cage, too. You'll need to be around to care-

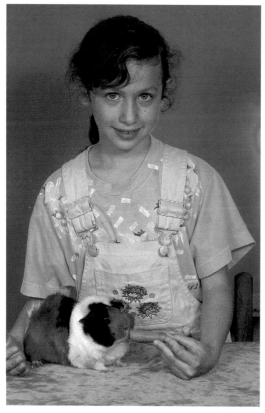

Is anyone in your family allergic to the animal you have chosen? Make sure the answer is no before you bring the pet home.

fully supervise this free-run time, and your house should be appropriately pet-proofed so it's safe for the animal.

Most of these small animals must gnaw on things or their teeth (which grow continuously their entire lives) will become too long. Overgrown teeth can result in serious health problems for any of these animals. A ferret's teeth don't grow, but most ferrets love to chew anyway.

And lastly, each of these pets needs veterinary care. Any living creature can become ill, and these small animals deserve appropriate care just like a larger, more expensive pet would. But sometimes, a vet who deals with these types of small mammals isn't easy to find. For this reason, you might want to locate a veterinarian who deals with small mammals such as guinea pigs, hamsters, and so on before you purchase such a pet.

When you and your child have considered everything involved with pet ownership, take your time choosing the best pet for your family. Involve the child in purchasing the food, housing, and other items the pet will need before you purchase the pet. Then, once you do bring the pet home, it will mean less stress for everyone as the animal adjusts to his new family.

With the exception of hamsters, small mammals enjoy each other's company. Most will be happier if you obtain a companion for them of the same species.

Teacher Tip—Choosing a Pet for the Classroom

Parents aren't the only ones who can offer children the opportunity to experience a pet. If you're a teacher, you might want to provide your students with a classroom pet. The vast majority of teachers who have had animals in their classrooms have had great success, and most educators support pets for children. With classroom pets, children can learn to care for various domesticated animals and see firsthand how these animals rely on humans for care. Follow these tips for choosing appropriate pets for the classroom:

- Animals that are small and that can be housed in a cage are best.

- Make sure the animal can emotionally and physically withstand a lot of attention and handling.

- Choose only pets that can stay alone (at school) over the weekend.

- Do not choose a classroom pet that you (the teacher) cannot or will not want to take home yourself.

- Be sure your classroom temperature remains fairly constant, even in the evenings when school is not in session. You might need to ask the custodian if heaters and air conditioners are turned off in the evenings and on weekends.

- Choose pets that don't require a lot of special care.

- Don't just expect the children to know how to behave around pets or how to handle them. You'll have to teach this.

- Have children wash their hands before and after handling the classroom pet.

- All pets brought into the classroom should come from a reputable pet store or dealer. Wild animals carry any number of parasites and diseases. Those obtained from pet stores are usually bred in captivity and have been checked for diseases and parasites. It's also a good idea to have a veterinarian check any animal you plan to use in the classroom.

- Avoid animals with a tendency to bite.

A classroom pet can be a great learning opportunity for teacher and students alike. Make sure to follow some simple guidelines when choosing an appropriate pet.

Chinchillas

Several years ago, few people knew much about chinchillas. Today, chinchillas are becoming more and more popular as pets—even Martha Stewart owns several of these soft, furry little rodents! Extremely cute animals, often described as looking like a mixture of a rabbit and a squirrel, chinchillas are about eight inches long and four inches wide on average and have an extremely soft coat, a bushy tail, large eyes, big ears, long whiskers, and a round, chubby body. Chinchillas are extremely clean, have no natural odor, and are generally very healthy animals.

Chinchillas originally came from the Andes Mountains in South America (hence the thick furry coat), so they're used to cold, dry weather. They were brought to America in the 1960s and soon became popular pets. Because they are rodents, they love to gnaw at things to keep their ever-growing teeth trimmed.

The standard color of a chinchilla is gray with a white stomach. Other mutations that can be found are white and beige. Rarer colors such as brown, black, and violet are a little harder to find, but are often available from breeders (check small animal magazines). Pet stores that carry chinchillas usually have only the standard gray color.

Purchasing a Healthy Chinchilla

Buying a chinchilla at a young age (eight weeks to six months) is best. Make sure the animal's eyes are bright and shiny and not drippy. Watery eyes are a sign of health problems. Check the mouth to make sure the top teeth do not overlap the bottom ones. Both sets should be fairly straight. The chinchilla should not paw at his mouth when eating. There shouldn't be any wetness under his chin. Teeth

The standard color of a chinchilla is gray with a white stomach.

problems are a major threat to a chinchilla's well-being, so you want to be sure his teeth are in good condition. Also, choose an animal that is fairly active. Chinchillas in pet stores are generally asleep during the day, but once awakened they will become active. Give the chinchillas plenty of time to adjust. When approaching them for the first time, be sure to move slowly and talk quietly so as not to frighten them. After the door to the cage is opened, let the chinchilla take a few minutes to get used to you. He will sniff and nibble at your fingers. Nibbling is the chinchilla's way of showing affection.

Never grab a chinchilla by his fur, because chinchillas can release fur if they are caught.

Housing and Accessories

A chinchilla needs to be housed in a wire cage or he will eat his way out and escape. When picking out a cage, find one that gives your pet a comfortable amount of space. The minimum size cage for one chinchilla should be 28"L x 18"W x 16"H. The litter for the bottom of the cage should be pine chips or a natural litter. Never use cedar chips. Cedar could be deadly for a chinchilla. A condo with two or three levels and ramps can also be used, because chinchillas need to be able to climb, run around, and play. They have a lot of energy and need exercise. If your chinchilla is housed in a cage that is too small to play in and he is not allowed to run outside the cage, you will end up with a frustrated and unhappy pet. Make sure the wire of the cage is not painted or plastic-coated, because your chinchilla will chew the paint or plastic off. Once you have chosen a cage, keep the cage out of drafts during colder months and in a well-ventilated area in the warmer months. Keep your chinchillas out of direct hot sunlight. Heat prostration is a common problem when chinchillas get too hot. Also make sure there are no electrical wires near the cage. Your chinchilla will chew through them.

Your chinchilla will need some basic feeding equipment. A feeder that can be attached to the side of the cage works best, because the food won't be spilled or walked on. A water bottle with a metal drinking spout should also be placed on the side of the chinchilla's cage. Note that the chinchilla will chew a hole through a plastic bottle, so protect it if you hang it inside the cage (your local pet store should have total metal encasings for water bottles). If you attach the bottle on the outside of the cage, placing some wire mesh between it and the bottle will also help stop them from chewing through it. If you can find a glass bottle, this may save money in the long run. Chinchilla blocks (or pumice blocks) will help keep your pet's teeth short and straight.

When you select a pet chinchilla, friendliness and overall health are the most important considerations.

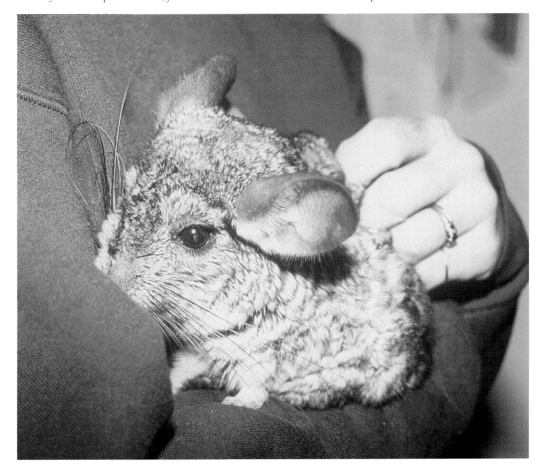

Feeding

A chinchilla's diet should consist mainly of fortified alfalfa pellets, specifically formulated for chinchillas. These are available at pet stores. A chinchilla will eat one to two tablespoons of the pellets daily. Make sure the food stays clean and fresh. You can supplement the chinchilla's diet with green vegetables, such as broccoli, lettuce, and celery. Don't offer too much watery food, however, because it can cause digestive problems. Fruit is fine as an occasional treat—most chinchillas seem to love raisins—but your chinchilla may develop a preference for the sugary taste if fruit is offered too often. Avoid high-fat foods, such as sunflower seeds and peanuts. Another suitable supplement is alfalfa or timothy hay, which will help satisfy the animal's need to gnaw and keep his teeth in good condition.

Basic Care

A chinchilla should also be kept clean and well groomed. Chinchillas love to take baths in special chinchilla dust made from volcanic ash. They dive and roll in the dust with great enthusiasm. Never put your chinchilla in real sand. Giving your chinchilla dust baths once or twice a week is sufficient. The dust may be reused, but droppings should be removed. Once the dust appears clumpy, replace it. Never wash chinchillas with water. The dust will help keep them clean and their fur soft.

To keep a happy and healthy chinchilla, make sure he gets plenty of exercise. A good way to provide your pet with the exercise he needs is to mount a chinchilla wheel inside the cage. Another way to allow your pet to exercise is to allow him to run around in a room that has been chinchilla-proofed. To chinchilla-proof a room, make sure that there are no wires within easy

A sizable one-story wire cage is adequate for your chinchilla, although a "condo" style with two or three levels is a better choice.

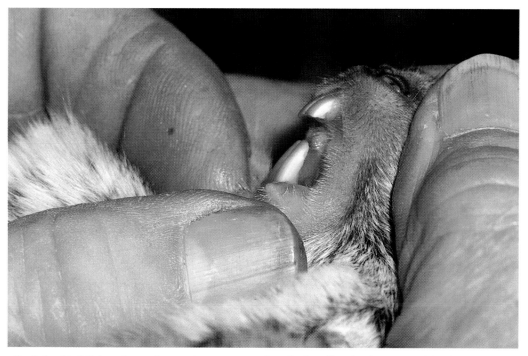

Check the chinchilla's teeth to make sure they are not misaligned. The yellowish color is normal for chinchillas.

access. Cover any holes through which your pet may escape. Pick up anything that may be harmful if the chinchilla eats it.

It's also best to keep your chinchilla in the house. If a chinchilla gets away from you outside, he will be very difficult to catch. Also, cats or other larger animals in the neighborhood may decide to make a meal of your pet.

What to Expect From a Chinchilla

Chinchillas are nocturnal. However, they will be active during the day if there is something interesting going on. They love to run on wheels, especially at night, so think twice before keeping your chinchilla in your child's bedroom. They are quite social animals and prefer to be kept in pairs or groups. They make noises to let you know you are not paying enough attention to them. Chinchillas hate change, prefer consistency, and do not like being moved much. If you move them, give them time to get used to the new surroundings.

Chinchilla Clubs

California Chins
2501 Cowper St.
Palo Alto, CA 94301
(650) 328-8296
E-mail: chinmom@aol.com
Web: www.cachins.com

Mutation Chinchilla Breeders Association, Inc.
(215) 679-5326
E-mail: mcbaweb@aol.com
Web: members.aol.com/
mcbaweb/mcbaorg.htm

National Chinchilla Breeders of Canada
RR 2 Norval
Ontario, Canada LOP 1K0
E-mail: ncbs@idirect.com
Web: www.chinnet.com/ncbc.html

Ferrets

A more exotic pet, and one best suited for an older child (at least eight years old), is the ferret. The domestic ferret is a member of the weasel family (polecat, mink, skunk, ermine, otter, etc.) and is a carnivore. Ferrets were domesticated before the cat, probably by the Egyptians. The first ferrets came to the US more than 300 years ago on ships and were used for rodent control.

Ferrets come in a variety of colors, with albino believed to be the original color of domesticated ferrets. Other popular colors are the naturally occuring sable (with a raccoon-like mask), chocolate, silver, and cinnamon. Patterns include mitts (white feet), panda (white head), badger (white blaze), and Siamese (dark legs and tail). Male ferrets are referred to as "hobs" and weigh an average of two to five pounds. Female ferrets are called "jills" and are half the size of the males. Baby ferrets are called "kits." A group of ferrets is called "a business of ferrets."

Ferrets have various scent glands for marking their territory and protecting themselves. Most pet stores sell ferrets that have been descented, which means the anal scent gland has been surgically removed. However, ferrets have various scent glands, called sebaceous glands, all over their bodies, so they always have a somewhat musky scent. Most people aren't bothered by this scent if the animal and its bedding, toys, and so on are kept clean. Ferrets reach adulthood at around six months and live an average of seven to nine years.

Purchasing a Healthy Ferret

Depending on where you live, ferrets may be completely legal, require a license to breed but not to own, require a permit to own, or be entirely illegal. This varies by state or province, county, and city. You can find out about your town by calling the local Wildlife Department or Fish and Game

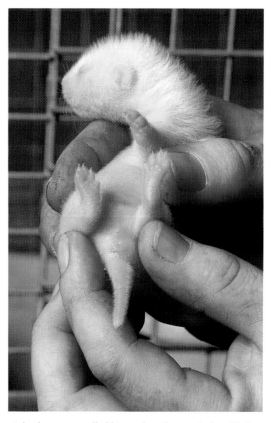

Baby ferrets are called kits and are born naked and helpless. They begin to grow fur shortly after birth.

Department, the humane society, or veterinarians. Note that some pet stores in towns where ferret ownership is illegal still sell ferrets, so don't rely on the availability of ferrets as an indication that they are legal to own in your area.

Always purchase a ferret from a reputable retailer, ferret rescue group, shelter, or breeder. The person selling the animal should be able to tell you its past health history as well as the history of the animals living with and around it and be willing to guarantee that the ferret is healthy.

When selecting a ferret, watch the litter at play. Be sure to choose an animal whose eyes and nose are clear, because the state of a ferret's eyes and nose are a good indication of his general health. Choose a ferret that is alert, playful, and friendly, but not the most boisterous one of the litter. This one may prove to be hard to handle as he grows older. As soon as you purchase a ferret, have him examined

Choose a pet ferret that is alert, playful, and friendly, but not the most boisterous one of the litter.

by your veterinarian. Ferrets need to be vaccinated against canine distemper and rabies and will always need annual booster shots. Whether you choose a male or female ferret, you should have your pet neutered or spayed. Most are sold with this already done. Neutering a ferret will often improve his disposition as well as reduce odor, and it is especially important for a female ferret because an unspayed female can become fatally ill if she is not bred when in heat.

Housing and Accessories

A suitable cage with an escape-proof latch is an absolute must for housing your ferret. While aquariums make fine homes for many other small mammals, they are not large enough and don't allow adequate ventilation for ferrets. Large, two to three-story cages are ideal. Cages should be at least 30 to 36 inches long, 16 to 18 inches wide, and a minimum of 18 inches high per floor. Washable pet rugs or towels are needed for the inside of the cage, because ferret paws are not designed to walk on wire floors.

The ferret's cage should be kept in a cool, shaded, dry area away from direct sunlight. Ferrets have few sweat glands, and these are poorly developed. They cannot tolerate temperatures above 80° F (26.5° C). Depending on their age, ferrets sleep between 15 and 20 hours a day; therefore, a comfortable sleeping area is important. Pet blankets, hammocks with synthetic lambswool centers, and small pet beds such as sleeping bags lined with synthetic lambswool are best. Cedar or pine chips should not be used for bedding because they present a respiratory risk to ferrets. Pelleted litter products made from recycled newspapers or plant fibers are good because they are super-absorbent, dust-free, and nonal-

Training Your Ferrets to Use the Litter Box

Ferrets aren't like cats, which naturally use a litter box. Try these tips for training your ferrets to use a litter box:

✔ Use a dust-free litter. Avoid clumping sand and scented litters. Place a little bit of soiled litter back into the clean pan to discourage kits from using the litter box as a sand or play box. Note: Do not use cedar or wood shavings in a ferret's cage. These can cause respiratory problems.

✔ Use a high-corner litter box designed for ferrets in the cage that covers at least two corners, and secure it in place so that the ferret cannot rearrange its location or tip it over. Make sure the litter box is large enough for the ferret's whole body—some corner pans are too small for a full-grown male ferret. The front of the litter box should be low enough to allow easy access for young ferrets.

✔ Make sure the ferrets are using the litter box in the cage well before giving them free run of a room. Place litter boxes in their chosen corners or use newspaper in the hard-to-reach or smaller areas.

✔ When you take them out to play, wake them up and cuddle with them for five minutes, put them back into the cage, and insist that they use the litter box.

✔ Allow free-run time in two-hour stages. Put the ferrets back in their cage to rest and use the litter box, then let them out again.

✔ Use newspaper where litter boxes won't work (under furniture, beds, behind doors, etc.) Paper-training your ferret is a little easier than box-training outside the cage, and newspaper is quick and easy to pick up and dispose of.

✔ Clean the litter boxes with dishwashing detergent—nothing harsh. Always save a little old litter to put back in a clean box if the ferret is still in the digging stage.

Adult ferrets sleep about 15 hours a day and are most active in the morning and evening.

lergenic. Scoopable clay litters are not recommended for ferrets. The materials from these litters may cause the ferret's coat to become dry and brittle, and constantly inhaling the dust may cause upper respiratory irritation.

Ferrets can be litter-trained in a small confined area such as a cage, but effective training requires appropriate litter products, technique, time (three to four weeks), positive reinforcement, and lots of patience.

Ferrets should not be left in any cage, no matter how roomy, for an extended period of time. They need plenty of exercise, love, and companionship on a daily basis, but because they can get into anything and everything, they need to be closely monitored when outside of their cage.

Soft latex or rubber cat and dog toys are not safe for ferrets because they like to chew on and swallow them. These types of toys are a major cause of intestinal blockage in ferrets and could possibly lead to the ferret's death. Cat teaser toys attached to strings on poles and washable cat crinkle tunnels and bags are much safer toys for ferrets. Small pet tents provide a fine place for ferrets to play and nap.

Feeding

Ferrets must be fed a premium dry ferret food with a meat-based protein and high fat content. Low ash, low fiber, and low magnesium are important to a good ferret diet as well. Ferrets have a very high metabolism, so they need constant access to food and water. They love to

Albino is believed to be the original color of domesticated ferrets, although sable is the natural color of wild ferrets.

snack on other foods, including some fruits and vegetables; however, they digest fiber poorly. Treats should be chopped into tiny pieces and given in small amounts not exceeding one teaspoon per day. Remember, this is a treat and not an alternative to quality food. Some acceptable snacks are melon (no seeds), sugar- and salt-free oat cereals, broccoli, or peeled cucumber.

Ferrets should not be left in any cage, no matter how roomy, for an extended period of time. They need plenty of daily exercise, love, and companionship.

Ferret Clubs

American Ferret Association
P.O. Box 255
Crownsville, MD 21032
(301) 663-6616
E-mail: afa@ferret.org
Web: www.ferret.org

California Domestic Ferret Association
P.O. Box 1991
Los Altos, CA 94023-1991
(650) 917-0346
E-mail: communications@cdfa.com
Web: www.cdfa.com

Ferret Fanciers Club
711 Chautauqua Ct.
Pittsburgh, PA 15214
(412) 322-1161

Ferret Unity & Registration Organization
Box 844
Elon College, NC 27244

Georgia Ferret Association
6326 Lively Way
Cumming, GA 30130
(404) 442-5917
E-mail: gfainc89@aol.com

Great Lakes Ferret Association
27654 South Pointe
Gross Ile., MI 48183
(313) 676-9138

United Ferret Organization
P.O. Box 606
Assonet, MA 02702
(508) 644-5562
E-mail: defret@aol.com

Ferrets, like rabbits, may be litter-trained with effort and patience.

Cooked egg and cooked meat scraps are healthy treats. Ferrets should NOT be fed dog food, sweets, salty foods, vegetarian or cat food diets, or bones. Ferrets should also never be given any chocolate, because it is very toxic to them. They are lactose-intolerant, so do not feed them milk, ice cream, cheese, or other dairy products. Heavy ceramic or weighted food bowls are recommended for ferret dishes, because ferrets like to tip things over. A 16-ounce water bottle should be secured to the outside of the cage, with the spout facing in. Water should be changed daily.

Basic Care

Of all small mammals sold for domestic pets, ferrets are perhaps the most expensive to buy and maintain and require the most daily care and attention, yet they are very loving, intelligent, and playful. They have the outgoing personality of a dog but are more mischievous and need to be watched more closely.

Ferrets should have access to food at all times.

Remove droppings from the litter box each day. If the litter box is not kept clean, the ferret will stop using it, so thoroughly wash and dry it at least once a week and fill it with clean litter. Wash your ferret's bed once a week. Also, clean out the cage every three to four days or once a week—remove all bedding material, thoroughly wash and dry the cage, then replace the bedding materials.

Once a month, bathe your ferret with special ferret shampoo to control his natural odors. Make sure to rinse him well. Trim your ferret's nails about once a month.

What to Expect From a Ferret

Adult ferrets sleep around 15 hours a day and are most active in the morning and evening. They usually coordinate their sleeping habits to conform to their owner's schedule. They will be awake when you're ready for breakfast and go back to sleep while you're at work and your child is at school, then be awake and ready to play when you get home again.

Although a ferret sleeps many hours a day, when he is awake, he is very active and curious. He likes to run around and play and often mischievously attacks household plants, steals socks, and pushes things off shelves. A ferret likes to hide whatever he can steal and usually puts things in a place he considers safe and convenient, which means he will generally have one or more secret stashes in your home. Discover these stashes, and you'll probably find anything that's been missing around the house.

Ferrets enjoy rough-and-tumble play with each other, which includes playful nipping. They will need to learn that they cannot be as rough with you or your child. A ferret should never be physically punished for nipping, because that will make him nervous and he may bite out of fear.

Ferrets are extremely sociable and love to have playmates. How well they get along with other domesticated animals depends on the personality and age of each. The introduction process should be slow and supervised at all times.

Ferrets are inquisitive, fearless, and capable of getting into places you never imagined. Be careful where you sit and walk when the ferret is out of his cage—he might be under a pillow, blanket, or pile of laundry. Never allow your ferret outdoors unless on a halter and leash and under close supervision.

When ferrets are nervous, scared, or exploring new territory, they often exhibit a characteristic known as the "bottle-brush tail." When this occurs, the tail gets big and puffy and the hair sticks straight out in a very silly fashion. This is a normal ferret reaction to environmental stimuli and does not mean your ferret is sick. It usually lasts only a few minutes, and then the tail will return to normal.

Web Sites for Ferret Lovers

Try these Web sites for more information about ferrets:

Electronic Zoo/NetVet Ferret Page

netvet.wustl.edu/ferrets.htm

This site contains a listing of links to other sites and other helpful information for ferret owners, including a link to the American Ferret Association, Inc., the California Domestic Ferret Association, and ferret lovers' clubs throughout the country.

Ferret Central

www.ferretcentral.org

This site includes frequently asked questions (FAQ) about ferrets, veterinary information, a photo gallery of ferrets, and links to a mailing list of ferret owners.

Ferret FAQ Global Index

www.next.com/Homes/dennis/~dennis/ff/faq-index.html

Questions and answers about every aspect of the care, feeding, and raising of ferrets. The site also provides links to many other sites and FAQs about behavior, health care, and keeping ferrets as pets.

Ferret Net

Here you can find out how to get on a ferret mailing list—either an international list or a regional list.

Gerbils

Gerbils are another excellent choice for your child's first pet because they're easy to care for and don't create much of a mess. Gerbils are slightly smaller than hamsters. They are about four inches long, with a flexible, fur-covered tail that is also about four inches long. There are about 89 species of gerbil, but the most common pet species is the Mongolian gerbil. Mongolian gerbils are natives of northeastern China and eastern Mongolia. It was not until the first half of the 1950s that Mongolian gerbils were imported into the US. They were first used as laboratory animals. In 1964, Mongolian gerbils were first imported into the UK. Mongolian gerbils have been very popular as pets since the early 1970s.

Gerbils are clean, nearly odorless, easy to feed and house, and naturally active during the day (which is rare among rodents). The basic color of a gerbil's coat is a golden brown with black ticking or stripes. Gerbils have superb hearing, and they love to jump, both from high levels and from the ground up.

Purchasing a Healthy Gerbil

When purchasing a gerbil, make sure that the animal seems naturally curious. At the pet store, if the gerbils are awake when you and your child approach their cage, they should come up to the side of the cage to see what is happening. When picked up, a gerbil should be curious and try to investigate, provided you have it in a stable position. The gerbil's eyes should be large and clear, the fur soft, and the tail as long as the body with a tuft of fur at the end. The body should be well-

When picked up, a healthy gerbil should be curious and try to investigate.

formed and stocky. Avoid purchasing a gerbil that has bites on his body or that nips at you. This may indicate overcrowding or a bad disposition. Look closely for a depressed, listless gerbil or one that has diarrhea. Make sure the animal does not have a sore, red, or bleeding nose. This usually means an infection or allergy to the bedding in the cage. Dry or ruffled fur and runny or dull eyes may also indicate that the animal is sick. Sometimes a healthy animal will be depressed if he has been alone for too long. If he perks up when you pick him up and his fur and eyes look good, then he is probably healthy.

Gerbils are highly social and do not like being alone. If you choose a gerbil for your child's first pet, you should get at least two. Lone gerbils have been proven to live shorter, less healthy lives and are often overweight and unhappy. They also tend to be harder to tame and less friendly. Plenty of human contact does not make up for the fact that a gerbil must eat alone and sleep alone, so a companion is essential. Both females and males will get along happily in same-sex pairs, especially if they are siblings or kept together from the age of six to eight weeks old.

Gerbils are hardy animals. With proper diet and care, a gerbil will live as long as three or four years.

Please note that it is not legal to keep gerbils in some areas. Check the laws by contacting your local Department of Wildlife, Department of Agriculture, Department of Natural Resources, or other governmental body responsible for implementing laws related to species that may be kept as pets in your area.

Housing and Accessories

Gerbils are very active little creatures and need plenty of space to move around. A glass aquarium makes an excellent home for gerbils, as long as it is large enough. A 20- or 30-gallon aquarium is ideal, but 10 gallons is the absolute minimum size. Be sure a fine wire mesh lid is fitted to the aquarium. This will keep your pet safely in his home but will still allow for proper air circulation. A cage can also be a good home for gerbils, as long as the bars are close enough together so the gerbils can't squeeze out. The bottom of the cage should be solid, not wire or mesh. A cage will be somewhat messier than an aquarium because gerbils tend to throw out some of the bedding and floor covering of their home as they burrow. Avoid enclosures made of wood because the gerbils will quickly gnaw through the wood and escape. Wood is also more difficult to keep clean.

Provide plenty of nesting material or litter for your gerbils, because they will rearrange the litter almost daily to make nests. The most important thing to remember about bedding and litter material is not to use cedar. Cedar contains highly volatile oils that can cause health problems for small animals that have to live in and breathe the fumes over an extended period of time. Pine is usable, but it has similar oils as cedar (along with all soft woods). Use only kiln-dried pine, because it has been baked in order to release the oils from the wood. Aspen shavings are much better. Gerbils will want soft materials to use to make their nests. You can purchase commercial nesting materials, but tissue paper or used paper also works well. Tear the paper into strips and crumple it. The gerbils will make a nest all by themselves. Don't use cotton or wool products for nesting materials because gerbils might ingest some of it.

Gerbils are very social animals and should not be kept alone. Two or more gerbils are no more trouble than one.

A large glass aquarium with a wire mesh lid makes an excellent home for gerbils because they love to dig and kick their bedding around.

Gerbils adjust well to almost any environment, but the ideal temperature is from 50 to 68° F (10 to 20° C). For lower temperatures, add extra nesting material. At extreme temperatures, gerbils become less active but are great explorers and climbers otherwise. It's best to keep the gerbil cage or aquarium away from the television and stereo speakers (loud noises are stressful to gerbils), drafts, direct sunlight, radiators, and heating or air-conditioning vents.

Feeding

Feed your gerbil once a day—the same time each day is best. Prepackaged pellets or gerbil seed mixes are available at pet stores. About one tablespoon per day of dry food is sufficient. You should supplement these with fresh vegetables and, if you wish, small insects like crickets, wax worms, and mealworms. Fresh veggies give the gerbil some extra moisture and vitamins, and gerbils enjoy them. Insects provide additional protein. Gerbils are not hoarders and will not overeat if fed too much. Sunflower seeds are a favorite treat. Make sure your gerbils have eaten everything you have placed in their dishes before giving them any more. This prevents the gerbils from just picking out sunflower seeds, corn, and other high-fat foods and leaving the higher-protein, lower-fat foods behind. For healthy adult gerbils, look for food with a moderate protein content (about 12 percent) and a fat content between 6 and 8 percent. Try to have as much of a variety of foods as possible to be sure that the gerbils are getting all the nutrients they need. Gerbils enjoy mineral blocks, which provide them with needed salts and minerals, so have one of these blocks in the cage at all times. Gerbils must also have a constant source of fresh water, so a drop bottle is ideal for the cage.

Basic Care

Gerbils take only a few minutes to feed and care for each day. Simply remove any old food from the cage, wipe out the food bowl, and put about a tablespoon (per gerbil) of food into the bowl. Empty and refill the water bottle each day, even if the gerbils don't drink all the water. Once a week, clean the bottle and check it for leaks.

Gerbils need a clean, dry home. Change the litter or bedding material every 10 to 14 days and thoroughly wash and dry the cage or tank before adding new litter.

Gerbils also need personal attention and exercise every day. You'll need to be around to supervise your child when he or she takes the gerbils out of the cage and plays with and handles them for at least 15 minutes a day. Gerbils also need about 30 minutes a day to run around freely outside of the cage without being picked up. Even children who are too young to handle a gerbil carefully without accidentally squeezing him too tightly will enjoy the entertainment provided by simply watching two or more of these cute little creatures as they play and exercise in their cage or other enclosure. Children as young as three can help care for gerbils by placing prewashed fruit and vegetables in the feeding bowl. Older children can help cut up and wash the fruit and vegetables, clean the bowl and water bottle, and even help wash out the cage.

What to Expect From a Gerbil

Gerbils are friendly, playful, and energetic. They respond well to humans when they're handled regularly. However, children under the age of seven need supervision when playing with them. Because gerbils are so active, an excited child can easily drop or squeeze a gerbil too hard. With supervision, very young children can pet the gerbils while they remain inside their cage without picking them up and watch them as they dig, burrow, and run around their enclosure. An older child should pick up the gerbil by letting him climb onto his or her hand or by scooping him up under his tummy. Have your child practice picking up the gerbil in his cage before taking him out. Never pick up the gerbil by his tail, but because gerbils may try to get away as you hold them, hold the base of the tail (not the tip) with one hand and cradle the gerbil's body in the palm of your other hand.

Your choice of bedding material is important. Avoid cedar and pine shavings, and use aspen or paper-based products instead.

Guinea Pigs

An excellent pet for children aged seven years and up is a guinea pig. A guinea pig is somewhat larger than a hamster, gerbil, or mouse, but it is still a rodent, also called a cavy (pronounced K-V). A female cavy is called a "sow" and a male cavy is called a "boar." Guinea pigs originated in the Andes Mountains region of South America. They were probably first domesticated by the Indians of Peru, who used them for food and as sacrificial offerings to their gods. In the 16th century, Dutch explorers introduced guinea pigs to Europe.

Guinea pigs are popular pets for many reasons. They are easily available at most pet stores, have an easygoing temperament, don't usually bite or scratch when handled, and are easy to care for. In their natural habitat, guinea pigs live in open, grassy areas. They look for shelter in naturally protected areas or burrows deserted by other animals. Guinea pigs are sociable animals and tend to live in groups. They are strictly herbivorous (plant-eating) and do most of their foraging for grasses, roots, fruits, and seeds in the late afternoon and early evening.

Guinea pigs are about eight inches long and weigh about two pounds as adults. They typically live about five years, although eight years is possible.

There are about 12 breeds of guinea pig you can choose from, with a number of color and patterns and hair types—normal, short-haired, long-haired, rough-coated, and rex (which looks somewhat like a teddy bear). Short-haired or rough-coated breeds are best as housepets, because the long-haired breeds require considerable grooming to keep their coats in good condition.

Guinea pigs are strictly plant-eating animals. In the wild, they do most of their foraging for grasses, roots, fruits, and seeds in the late afternoon and early evening.

Purchasing a Healthy Guinea Pig

Guinea pigs should be at least four to six weeks old before they are purchased, so they are fully independent of their mother. Choose a healthy-looking, energetic guinea pig with no signs of disease. If you try to pick up the guinea pig and he shows very little interest, there's something wrong—a healthy guinea pig will usually either run away from your hand or investigate it.

Housing and Accessories

When selecting housing for your guinea pigs, you'll need at least 2 square feet of floor space per animal, and the enclosure should be at least 15 inches high. The floors should have a solid bottom and the sides may be wire or solid. Wire floors should not be used for a guinea pig, because the animal can get his toenail, or even the entire foot, caught in the mesh. If you are keeping your guinea pig in a fairly warm, draft-free area, a wire-sided cage is fine—however, the animal will constantly push bedding out of the cage and onto the table or floor as he makes his bed, so this type of enclosure can be quite messy. Use wood shavings, either fir or white pine, for bedding. There are many types of commercial bedding available in pet stores, but these can prove to be rather costly. Wood shavings can be purchased in a 40-pound paper bale and are relatively inexpensive. These bales can be found at farm stores, feed dealers, and garden centers. When buying these bales, be sure to specify "small animal" bedding, because these shavings are graded according to size. Do not use cedar shavings as bedding. Many rodents, including guinea pigs, are sensitive to the cedar oils, which may cause problems such as runny eyes, discharge from the nose, and skin irritations. Avoid using bedding that contains very fine particles and dust. If you run out of bedding, shredded newspaper can be used in emergencies.

Ideal temperatures for the guinea pig range from 65 to 75° F (18 to 24° C) with 50 percent humidity. Guinea pigs can tolerate temperatures as low as 60° F (16° C) and as high as 90° F (32° C) without suffering any ill effects. Sudden extreme changes of temperature should be avoided.

Feeding

A guinea pig's main diet should consist of dried timothy hay or another grass

An ideal guinea pig cage provides at least two square feet of space per animal and is at least 15 inches high.

hay like alfalfa, supplemented by pellets and fresh vegetables. Keep your guinea pig's bowl filled with fresh pellets daily. Guinea pig pellets contain vitamin C because guinea pigs cannot synthesize vitamin C from food and must have it added to their diet. When buying pellets, make sure they have not been on the shelf more than 90 days. After 90 days, the quality of the vitamin C is minimal. Another important point to consider when buying pellets is the protein level. Guinea pigs

Most fresh vegetables and fruits that are safe for humans are safe for guinea pigs.

A guinea pig's main diet should consist of dried timothy or alfalfa hay along with pellets and fresh vegetables. Constant access to water is very important.

need at least an 18 percent protein level in their pelleted feed in order to stay healthy. Most guinea pig pellets are 18 to 20 percent protein. Another easy way to add vitamin C to the pig's diet is to put it in his water: 100 soluble milligrams per cup of drinking water, made fresh daily.

Guinea pigs should get a cup or two of fresh vegetables daily—aim for those that are high in vitamin C and other nutrients. Most fresh vegetables and fruits that are safe for humans are safe for guinea pigs.

A heavyweight crock that the animal cannot tip over is ideal for pelleted feed. The dish should not be so large that the guinea pig decides it would make a great place to sit or sleep. An open crock should not be used as a water container. Because guinea pigs like to run around their cage, the water would soon be unfit to drink. A water bottle with a ball-bearing tip is ideal. The size of the bottle you need depends on how many animals are housed in

Guinea pigs need to be allowed to run around outside the cage to get some extra daily exercise.

one cage. An 8-ounce bottle will serve one guinea pig, while a 16-ounce bottle can serve two or three.

Basic Care

As far as small pets go, guinea pigs are among the easiest to care for. You will need to feed them, check their water daily, and change their bedding about once or twice a week—somewhat less when they are small. They also need to be allowed to run around a larger area for exercise each day.

Clean the cage at least once a week. Wash and disinfect the feed crock and water bottle once a week. Most importantly, give the guinea pig lots of love and attention on a daily basis.

You will probably need to trim your guinea pig's toenails, unless the animal does a lot of

running around on bricks or concrete or other rough surfaces that will keep the nails short. Nails that are not clipped will eventually curl back into the pad of the foot, crippling the guinea pig, or break off, sometimes causing bleeding and infection. You can clip the nails at home yourself or have a vet do it.

What to Expect From a Guinea Pig

When you bring your guinea pig home, he may be frightened and unsure of his surroundings. He may not eat or drink much the first few days, and when you or your child enter the room the animal may run to a corner of his cage to hide. After he gets to know you and realizes who is feeding him, he will squeal and squeak when he sees you.

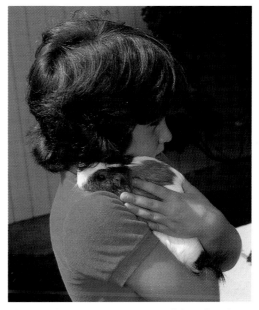

If your child treats her guinea pig well, he will probably become very tame.

Guinea pigs are sociable creatures and are usually a lot happier with company. If you don't have a lot of time to spend with your guinea pig or are gone for much of the day, your guinea pig may be a lot happier if you get him or her a friend. Same-sex groups, of either sex, usually get along fine if there is adequate room. And, of course, sexes should be separated or you'll soon end up with a constant supply of new guinea pigs.

Remember, even a child is very large and frightening to a guinea pig. Also, being picked up is very scary to them, because guinea pigs can't really climb or jump—they like to stay on the ground. It's probably best if you lift the guinea pig from his cage and have your child sit down before he or she holds the pet. The best way to pick up a guinea pig is to place one hand under the belly and lift. Then, as soon as the animal is off the ground, place another hand under the hind legs so the guinea pig feels secure and supported. Put the animal in your child's lap—maybe on a towel so you don't have to worry about accidents—and let the child pet him. This is a good time to give fresh vegetable treats, so the pet learns to enjoy the experience. As soon as the guinea pig begins to squeak or become restless, take the guinea pig from your child and put the pig back in his enclosure.

Guinea Pig Clubs

American Cavy Breeders Association
   22859 Fall Leaf Rd.
   Linwood, KS 66052
   Web: acba.osb-land.com

Columbia River Rabbit & Cavy Breeders Association
   (503) 257-8550

Guinea Hog Association
   14335 Pauma Vista Dr.
   Valley Center, CA

Oregon League of Rabbit & Cavy Breeders
   26730 SE Currin Rd.
   Estacada, OR 97023

Hamsters

Hamsters make an ideal first pet for children because they're small in size, relatively inexpensive, and don't require a lot of time out of their cages. Their housing is also easy to keep clean. Hamsters are friendly and tame if they are treated well. Hamsters are cute and cuddly, with short legs and a small tail. They have large cheek pouches that extend down over their shoulders. In the wild, these pouches are used to store food to carry back to their nests, which helps the animals survive in times when food is scarce.

According to scientists, there are more than 24 species of hamster, but only 4 are popular as pets. The Syrian or golden hamster is the best known. Syrian hamsters are so named because they originated in a small area of northwestern Syria. The Syrian hamster was brought to the United States in 1938, but did not become popular until the late 1940s and 1950s.

The Syrian hamster has a short, roly-poly body measuring about 6.5 inches (16 cm) long. He weighs about 4 ounces (113 g). Syrian hamsters come in many colors—the original golden, cinnamon, rust, dark gray, light gray, yellow, cream, black, and even tortoiseshell. These hamsters are also available in a number of different coat types, including short-haired, long-haired (known as Teddy Bear), rex (curly), and satin. Syrian hamsters usually live about two years.

In recent years, three species of dwarf hamster have steadily gained in popularity—the Russian dwarf hamster, Roborovski's dwarf desert hamster, and the Chinese hamster. All of these are half the size of the Syrian hamster.

The Russian dwarf hamster is about three to four inches long, with the female slightly smaller than the male. It has a short, wide head with tiny, round ears. Its tail is barely visible, and its feet are furred. The fur of the Russian dwarf hamster is thick with a dense undercoat, and

Hamsters make an ideal first pet for children because they're small in size, relatively inexpensive, and don't require a lot of time outside their cages.

the natural color is brownish-gray with a gray undercoat. This hamster comes in a number of colors including normal, albino, argent, opal, and platinum; and two coat types, normal and satin.

Roborovski's hamster is found in the wild in western and southern Mongolia and northern China. It is the smallest pet dwarf hamster—only about two inches long. Roborovski's hamster has large round eyes and very soft fur. Its natural color is sandy, golden brown. The average life span of this hamster is two to three years, although it can live longer.

The Chinese hamster is long and slender and measures about three to four inches in length. Its tail is longer than the tails of other types of dwarf hamsters. Chinese hamsters are gray-brown, with a dark stripe that runs from between the eyes to the base of the tail. The average life span for Chinese hamsters is three years.

The Syrian hamster and the various dwarf hamsters make excellent pets, but dwarf hamsters tend to be friendlier than Syrian hamsters. Both varieties are nocturnal, but the Syrian hamster is more likely to become irritable if awakened during the day.

Purchasing a Healthy Hamster

Hamsters should be purchased when they are six to ten weeks old. By that time they no longer need their mother (the hamster will have been weaned at three weeks of age) but are still young enough to bond readily with your child. As single pets, males or unbred females are usually the best choice. Mother hamsters can be aggressive and may even bite. It's also important to realize that while dwarf hamsters are quite happy living in pairs or even groups, Syrian hamsters should be housed alone. Otherwise, they tend to become aggressive and fight quite frequently. If you notice any fighting among hamsters sharing a cage (even among dwarf hamsters), it's best to separate them into individual cages immediately.

Purchase your hamster from a reputable breeder or pet shop that sells only healthy animals and gives them the proper care they need. A healthy hamster will have dark eyes that are bold and bright. He'll also have a natural curiosity for things and be alert and responsive, not nervous or jumpy, when you approach him. A healthy hamster will have soft, silky fur with a bit of a sheen, and a plump, solid little body. His nose should be slightly damp, but not wet, and he should be eating well.

Housing and Accessories

A small cage will make a fine home for a hamster, but allow at least one square foot of space per animal. Avoid cages made of wood, because these tend to soak up urine and are harder to clean, and also because the animal can gnaw through the bottom of the cage in just a short time. You'll need some sort of litter material to line the bottom of the cage. Avoid cedar shavings, which can be harmful to small animals. Instead, use aspen or pine wood shavings or shavings manufactured from paper or pulp. Your hamster will also need bedding material so he can build a nest where he will sleep. Shredded paper, soft hay, sawdust, dry grass, or any other clean, absorbent material that provides plenty of ventilation works well. Avoid fluffy cotton, wool, or other man-made fibers for bedding. If the hamster eats any of this material it could cause intestinal blockage and eventually kill him. Put about a handful of bedding into the cage at a time.

Hamsters are private animals and enjoy a nest box where they can sleep and go for privacy. This isn't absolutely necessary, but it will make your hamster feel more secure. You can find a variety of nest boxes or hamster houses at pet stores.

Hamsters are also naturally active and will need toys—especially an exercise wheel—to keep them busy and allow them to get adequate exercise. Your child will enjoy shopping for these because there are so many colorful, appealing hamster toys on the market. However, if you purchase hamster gyms or play equipment, you should realize that these are hard to clean and should

Dwarf hamsters have steadily gained in popularity over the last few years. They are about half the size of Syrian hamsters.

not be left in the hamster's home all the time. Put them in the cage for a while each day, then remove and clean them.

Avoid placing water dishes or food dishes inside the cage. Hamsters tend to walk and urinate in their food if it's kept in their cage. Instead, choose a food hopper or feeding chute that opens into the cage.

Water bottles that can be hung outside the cage on a clip, with the spout inside the cage, are perfect for a hamster. That way, the hamster has constant access to water, but he won't spill it and soak his food, bedding material, or the inside of his cage.

Because hamsters are rodents, they will constantly chew on things to keep their ever-growing teeth trim, so a gnawing block of some sort is also a good item for the hamster's home.

Feeding

Hamsters are basically herbivores and enjoy a varied diet. Numerous commercially prepared hamster mixes are available at pet stores. These packaged foods contain such things as oats, corn, wheat, barley, and sunflower seeds. Rodent pellets may also be fed to your hamster, but you should still provide a hamster mix for variety. Small amounts of fresh fruits and vegetables can be offered as treats. You may give vitamins and other supplements to your hamster in his water supply if you wish. Read package directions carefully when you purchase these items.

Basic Care

Feed your hamster once a day, preferably at the same time each day. Evening is usually best, because that's when the hamster awakens. Always look in the cage for any hoarded food, which will eventually rot, and remove it. Empty and refill the water bottle each day and clean it at least once a week.

Hamsters are quite clean creatures and will always deposit their waste in just one spot of the cage, usually a corner. This makes partial cleaning easy—each day, remove soiled or damp litter and spot-

Elaborate plastic cages sold for hamsters can be expensive and hard to clean, but most hamsters really seem to enjoy them.

clean, if necessary. Once a week, remove all the litter and bedding material, thoroughly wash and dry the cage, and then put down new litter and bedding. Hamsters never need a bath, because they groom themselves much like cats do. You'll only need to groom your hamster if he is one of the long-haired varieties. These hamsters need to be brushed for five or ten minutes every day or so.

Hamsters' teeth and nails wear down naturally as they grow, so you won't need to bother trimming them unless something goes wrong.

Hamsters will hibernate if the temperature drops too low (below 60° F [16° C]), but do not let the temperature rise much above 75° F (24° C), which may create heat stress. Light, although not harmful, should not be constant, and your hamster should not be subjected to too much direct sunlight. Excessive dampness contributes to disease, and extreme cold can even cause the animal to go into hibernation, so keep the cage dry and warm.

What to Expect From a Hamster

Hamsters are gentle, trusting, and inquisitive. However, they need a little time to get used to handling, and children under the age of seven should always have adult supervision when taking their hamster from his cage and playing with him. Children may find it hard to understand that hamsters usually want to be left alone during the day. For this reason, it's best to encourage your child to develop a regular playtime with the hamster in the early evening or at night. Caution your child never to poke or frighten a sleeping hamster or try to wake him up suddenly, because the hamster might bite.

To pick up a hamster, slip one hand under his tummy and quickly cup your other hand over his back and in front of his face. Always hold the hamster with both hands. Because hamsters are wiggly and can suddenly jump out of your hands, it's best to have children sit down when they handle them. Also, remind your child not to squeeze the hamster.

Hamster Clubs

There are many groups dedicated to hamsters. Club members share information about their pets, and often these organizations sponsor shelters, shows, and exhibitions. For more information about any of the clubs listed here, write to them and include a self-addressed, stamped envelope for a reply.

The American Rat, Mouse & Hamster Society
13317 Neddic Ave.
Poway CA 92064-5108
(619) 748-5395

Chubby Cheeked Hamster Association
Aimee Strickland
12060 SE 112th Avenue Rd.
Belleview FL 34402
(352) 288-2297

Hamster Club of America
2931 South Fairview #C
Santa Ana, CA 92704
(714) 545-4715
E-mail: allivan@pacbell.net
Web: hca.hypermart.net

Hamster Fanciers of America
107 Savannah Drive W.
Bear, DE 19701-1635
(302) 836-1111
E-mail: ravena@geocities.com
or sampett@towerhill.org
www.geocities.com/heartland/hills/1327

Rat, Mouse & Hamster Fanciers
2309 Country Ranch Drive
Modesto CA 95355
E-mail: jstarkey@telis.org

Mice and Rats

Most people don't think of keeping mice or rats in their homes on purpose, but actually these animals were probably the first rodent species to be kept as pets. They're very clean, easy to care for, and love to interact with humans. A mouse weighs about one ounce and has a total length of about six inches, including his tail. A rat is somewhat larger, weighing about 14 ounces, with a total length of about 12 inches. In both animals, males are larger than females. Mice generally live one to two years, while rats tend to live about twice as long.

Both mice and rats are available in a wide range of colors and patterns. The mouse's coat type may be normal, satin, rex, or long-haired. The rat's fur may be normal or rex (curly). Both mice and rats make excellent pets for children if they are cared for properly. They seldom bite when raised as pets and handled with care.

These timid and social pets are fun to watch performing their natural behaviors of burrowing, searching for food, and playing. Unlike their wild counterparts, which are typically nocturnal, pet rats and mice have periods of activity both day and night.

Choosing a Healthy Mouse or Rat

Mice or rats may often be purchased when they're about four weeks old. Ideally, they should not leave the litter before five weeks of age. If you get them too young, they will be jumpy and hard to socialize at first. Some pet shops will offer mice for sale as soon as they start to eat solid food, at about two weeks of age. However, although mice this young eat solid food, they really need their mother's milk for another couple of weeks. Mice weaned this early often don't survive.

Rats are quite a bit larger than mice. They weigh about 14 ounces and are about 12 inches long.

Mice are not fully grown until at least 12 weeks of age, and many mice take longer than this to reach full size. It is best to keep two female mice (called "does") together, to provide company for each other. Two males will fight bitterly, and they also smell much stronger than females. A male and a female are not a good combination, because they will keep producing babies.

Mice are social animals, and it is very unnatural for them to live alone, so you'll need to buy at least two. Single mice are generally bored, lonely, and miserable, and they do not make good pets because they tend to spend a great deal of time sleeping or hiding in the nest box. With a single mouse, you also miss out on the fun of watching mice play together and groom each other.

Pet rats are usually obtained from a breeder or a pet shop. A good breeder or pet shop clerk will be able to give advice after you have taken the rats home and will usually take the rats back if you have any problems with them. Good rat breeders and good pet shops put a lot of time and effort into breeding and socializing pet rats. They will only breed from good-quality, healthy, friendly animals and will allow the mother to rest between litters. The babies will have been regularly handled from a young age, before their eyes have opened, and should be comfortable with humans by the

Aquariums or cages with narrow bars make suitable homes for mice and rats. Make sure the cage is big enough to allow for plenty of exercise.

time they are ready to leave home—not hiding away or urinating in fear when they are picked up. They will usually be over six weeks old and certainly no younger than five weeks. The breeder or pet shop should be able to tell you their date of birth. They will have no problem telling the sexes apart—rats can be easily sexed from a few days of age, with a little practice. They will have kept male and female rats separate from the age of five weeks, because females can become pregnant even at this age.

Good breeders and good pet shops will certainly care about the welfare of their animals and will want to make sure you have suitable housing and know how to keep rats before they will let you buy any from them.

As a pet for a child, it's best to choose the friendliest rat, not necessarily the cutest one in the bunch.

If you decide to get a mouse and a rat, don't keep them in the same cage.

Good rat breeders put a lot of time and effort into breeding and socializing pet rats. Youngsters like these 20-day-old rats will have been handled nearly from birth.

Housing and Accessories

Finding the appropriate enclosure for your mouse or rat is easy. You can find a wide variety of suitable cages at any pet store. Aquariums do not allow the best ventilation, but they are useful if you cannot find a cage with bars that are narrow enough. A cage should be at least 12 inches wide, 10 inches tall, and 20 inches long. It should be spacious enough for the animals to move about freely and should allow adequate ventilation. A solid floor is necessary to prevent hock or foot sores.

Line the cage with several inches of litter or nesting material (shredded aspen works well, but check to see what your pet store has available). As with other small mammals, cedar shavings should not be used.

Both rats and mice enjoy having a nest box for sleeping, so an enclosed space should be provided. A variety of hamster nest boxes are available at pet stores, and these can be used for mice or rats. As with the cage, these homes should be cleaned when they become soiled or dirty. Other accessories that keep your rodent

Tips for Choosing a Mouse or Rat at the Pet Store

✔ Wear old clothes when you go to pick out your pet. When an animal doesn't know you and is afraid, it's natural for him to have accidents, so it's best to be prepared.

✔ Bring a clean, old rag to the pet store. Many pet stores will put your rats in a cardboard box for you to take them home in. This box is new and scary, and the rat or mouse will slide all over the box if there is nothing else in it. A disposable piece of cloth gives the animal(s) something to hide in and hold onto.

✔ At the pet store, leave your hand in the cage for a while. One or two rats will probably come over to check you out. Speak softly and avoid sudden movements. Hold your hand open, palm up, and put a treat in your palm. You might want to take home the mouse or rat who chooses you.

friend happy include ladders, exercise wheels, and, of course, a constant supply of chewable items. Clean, non-toxic branches or twigs and cotton ropes can be added for hours of fun. It is best to rotate toys through the cage, never leaving a toy in so long that the animal becomes bored with his environment.

A mouse or rat's home should be kept dry and warm. Put the enclosure in an area with external temperatures in the range of 70 to 75° F (21 to 24° C), and quickly remove wet bedding or leaking water bottles.

Handle your pet rat as much as possible. He will soon learn to enjoy your company.

Feeding

As with any pet, good-quality food and clean, fresh water must be provided at all times. In the wild, these animals feed on leaves, seeds, roots, fruits, and insects. Pelleted rodent rations, which are processed as dry blocks or pellets, are recommended for feeding in captivity. Typical maintenance diets contain about 14 percent protein and 4 to 5 percent fat. Seed diets are also formulated for mice and rats, but these diets should only supplement the basic rodent pellet as a treat item. Rodents prefer sunflower seed-based diets to pellets, but these seeds are low in calcium and high in fat and cholesterol. When fed exclusively, seed diets can lead to obesity and nutritional deficiencies. The pet's appetite should be monitored closely. Many factors affect the rodent's food intake, including the surrounding temperature, humidity, food quality, breeding status, and the pet's health status.

Water should be provided in water bottles equipped with sipper tubes. The sipper tube keeps the water free from contamination. Although rodents drink only a fraction of the water in the bottle, the bottle should be emptied, cleaned, and refilled with fresh water daily.

Basic Care

Mice and rats are inexpensive and easy to care for, but they do require some daily attention. Mice should be fed twice a day on a regular schedule. Any old food should be removed first, the bowl washed out, and the new food put down. Every other day, the water bottle should be emptied, cleaned, and refilled. A small amount of fruit or vegetables should be offered to the mice every other day as well. The cage and accessories should be thoroughly cleaned at least once a week. More frequent cleaning may be necessary if you have several animals in a single cage. Every day, clean out the enclosure by removing any droppings (it's best to wear rubber gloves for this). Every other day, change the litter, and once a week thoroughly wash and dry the enclosure and put down fresh litter.

What to Expect From a Mouse or Rat

Mice and rats need frequent, gentle handling to teach them to trust and socialize with human beings. But because mice are so small and fragile, small, excitable children who could easily squeeze them too hard should not hold them. Usually, by the age of nine or ten, children are old enough to handle these pets carefully and quietly. Before that time, however, three or four mice in a large tank (20-gallon or larger) can be very entertaining for children to watch as the animals play with their toys. The more attention you give your new mice or rats when you first get them home, the sooner they will get used to your voice and your smell and begin to make friends with you. Handle your rats as much as possible, whether they seem to like it or not at first. They will soon learn to enjoy your company.

Rats and mice should not be picked up by the tail—they don't like it, and it can cause injury. It is best to lift your rats and mice by placing one or both hands under the chest, behind the front legs, but be careful not to squeeze!

Rats dislike loud noises and rough handling, so it is very important that children learn to handle rats carefully, under close supervision. A pet rat should never bite, but when scared by rough handling even the gentlest pet may try to defend himself. Like many animals, rats can be destructive if they are left unsupervised for long periods of time. You should make sure you know where your rats are at all times while they roam free in your house, and rat-proof any room they are let loose in. Electrical cords should be covered with aquarium tubing, which you'll find in most pet shops. Rats will also chew books, clothes, pencils, and other items and are liable to knock things over, so breakables and valuables should be put out of harm's reach while your rats are out of their cage. Make sure windows and doors are closed and there are no possible escape routes. Rats can fit through tiny holes, so check for cracks along skirting boards, between floorboards, etc. Some houseplants can be poisonous, and rats often enjoy climbing plants and digging in plant pots, so it is probably best to keep plants away from your rats.

As with most rodents, rats and mice are most active in the middle of the night, when you and your child are asleep. For that reason, you'll want to have two or more rats or mice to a cage to keep each other company. Rats or mice kept in pairs or groups are happier, more confident, and no more difficult to tame.

Rat and Mouse Clubs

American Rat, Mouse and Hamster Society
13317 Neddick Ave.
Poway, CA 92064-5108
(619) 748-5395

Rat and Mouse Club of America
(headquarters—
there are several local chapters, too)
13075 Springdale St. Suite 302
Westminster, CA 92683
(949) 631-4513
E-mail: rmcal@aol.com
Web: www.rmca.org

The Rat Fan Club
857 Lindo Ln.
Chico, CA 95973
(800) 728-5052
E-mail: ratlady@sunset.net
Web: www.ratfanclub.org

Rabbits

Not too long ago, rabbits were considered outdoor pets and were kept in hutches out in the yard. Today, rabbits have become popular housepets, and many live with the family more like a cat or dog. In fact, the House Rabbit Society, a national nonprofit organization, recommends that rabbits be kept in the house rather than outdoors because "they are intelligent, social animals that need affection and can become wonderful companion animals if given a chance to interact with their human families." However, the natural exuberance, rambunctiousness, and noise level of the average toddler is stressful for most rabbits, so they usually make the best pets for children seven years of age and older.

Unlike many other small mammals, the rabbit is not a rodent but a member of the related order *Lagomorpha*, which includes hares and pikas. There are about 47 species of rabbits and hares, and more than 70 rabbit breeds to choose from, some being much more popular and available than others. There are long-haired breeds (angora-types, which require more upkeep because their hair needs regular combing), normal-haired, and the rex breeds (whose coat has a plush, velvet-like texture). Ear carriage may be erect or floppy, and the ears may be long or short. The most popular breeds in the US are the Mini Rex, Netherland Dwarf, Holland Lop, Mini Lop, Jersey Wooly, Californian, Dutch, French Lop, and the American Fuzzy Lop. Each of these, with the exception of the Californian and the French Lop, is a small or dwarf breed. Depending on breed, rabbits can be as small as 2 1/2 pounds or as large as 14 pounds and up.

The long-haired angora breeds of rabbit require regular grooming and are probably not the best choice for inexperienced rabbit-keepers.

Purchasing a Healthy Rabbit

Take your time when shopping for a rabbit. You want to make sure you're buying a healthy pet, one that is right for your child. This little creature will be a member of your family for at least six or seven years and sometimes longer. A healthy rabbit will be alert and aware of his surroundings. He will hop around, and if you put your hand in the cage, he should show an interest. If the rabbit shies away, he may have been mistreated. If he sits in a corner with little concern about the sights and sounds around him, he may be sick. Check the rabbit's teeth before you buy. The top incisors should slightly overlap the bottom ones. They should be clean and shouldn't be cracked or broken. Look in the cage and make sure the rabbit's droppings are round and hard. The rabbit's feet should be clean, because a well-raised rabbit is brought up in a cage where he won't sit in his own excrement.

Young rabbits should not be taken from their mothers until they are at least six weeks of age. Pet stores and breeders usually will not sell young bunnies before this time, but be sure to ask anyway. If a rabbit is taken away from his mother and siblings prematurely, his digestive system is not fully developed. Rabbits have different personalities, so it is difficult to make generalizations about breeds, although some breeds tend to be more affectionate than others. In general, you'll find that a medium- to large-breed rabbit is usually better for a child. Dwarf breeds tend to be more excitable, energetic, and aggressive.

Housing and Accessories

Rabbits like to move around. They love to stretch in every direction, and although they may look rather small and compact in a normal sitting position, rabbits are surprisingly long creatures. For this reason, it is necessary to purchase the largest cage you can afford. At home, keep the cage away from heating and air-conditioning vents, direct sunlight, and loud appliances, as well as televisions and stereos. There are generally two types of cages available on the market: those with solid-tray bottoms and those with wire mesh bottoms and a tray underneath. Regardless of the cage you choose, put some straw in the bottom, which the bunny will use for bedding. If you purchase a cage with a wire bottom, put a wooden board or a bit of carpet in the cage. Otherwise, the wire mesh can be hard on the rabbit's feet and he may develop sore hocks. If you purchase a cage with a plastic tray, you must change the bedding very frequently, perhaps three times a week.

In nature, rabbits like to live in warm, dark burrows in the ground. To provide this same feeling of security and comfort for a domestic rabbit, buy or build a nest box. It should be constructed from thin plywood and should have a small entry hole cut into one side. If the roof of the box is hinged, cleaning is much easier.

Besides a comfortable cage and a nest box, your rabbit will need a place where he can run around

Signs of a Sick Bunny

Although rabbits are healthy and happy most of the time, they can occasionally become ill, just like any other living creature. But unlike humans, who can make their illness known by telling someone how they feel, rabbits usually suffer in silence unless the owner notices something is wrong. Here are some signs of a sick bunny. Call your veterinarian immediately if you notice any of these symptoms:

✔ Sudden loss of appetite with bloat and abdominal gurgling

✔ Diarrhea with listlessness

✔ Loss of appetite with runny nose

✔ Loss of appetite with labored breathing

✔ Head tilted

✔ Urine-soaked rear legs

✔ Lumps, bumps, or swelling anywhere on the body

✔ Any sudden behavior change

Young rabbits should not be taken from their mothers until they are at least six weeks of age. This cute little litter is still much too young.

and get some exercise each and every day. You can let the rabbit have the run of one or many rooms in your house, but you must first bunny-proof your home. This means covering wires, moving expensive wooden furniture, and so forth. Another idea is to build an indoor pen for your bunny, or even let him spend some time outdoors in the yard each day as long as it is fenced and you can be there to make sure he doesn't escape.

Feeding

The amount you feed your rabbit depends on his or her size, activity level, and age. An average six- to eight-pound rabbit will eat about one to one-and-one-fourth cups of food per day. Smaller dwarf rabbits will eat about half that amount per day. Keep in mind, though, that individual rabbits will have their own feeding requirements. If the rabbit does not eat the entire portion you offer, you are probably overfeeding him. Pay particular attention during feeding times to learn to gauge how much he eats. Dispense the food from a hopper or heavy ceramic bowl, because rabbits are generally rambunctious creatures that delight in sitting in their food or overturning their dishes. Rabbits should be fed twice a day, at the same times every day—morning and evening. A rabbit's diet should comprise quality pellets, mixed rabbit food (cereals and seeds), fresh green goods and fruits, and ample fresh hay. Carrot tops and lettuce, as well as fruits including apples, pears, and

A healthy rabbit will be alert and aware of his surroundings. He will hop around, and if you put your hand in the cage, he should show an interest.

bananas can be offered as occasional treats, but only in moderation. Avoid giving these to young rabbits, because they can be prone to stomach upsets if anything but a proper, well-balanced diet is offered before the gastrointestinal tract has fully developed. Rabbits also need access to fresh, clean water at all times. A thirsty rabbit won't eat. Under normal conditions, rabbits need to drink approximately one-fourth cup of water per pound of body weight per day. In warmer weather, be sure to have extra water available to your rabbit at all times. Water bottles have an advantage over dishes because the water is always fresh and does not get dirty.

Rabbits are especially prone to gastric hairballs because they lack the natural ability to vomit, and

Place some straw in the bottom of the cage, along with a wooden resting board. Otherwise, the wire mesh can be hard on the rabbit's feet.

Rabbits need to have access to fresh, clean water at all times. They will drink about one-fourth cup of water per pound of body weight per day.

the opening from a rabbit's stomach to the small intestine is very small. Rabbits with hairballs will stop eating and produce fewer droppings. Extra fiber in the diet can help with hairballs by attaching to the hair to aid in flushing the hair out of the stomach.

Basic Care

Clean the rabbit's food bowl every morning, then put down new pellets, vegetables, and fresh timothy or alfalfa. In the evening, replenish the hay and vegetables and refill the water bottle. Every couple of days, you should give the rabbit some fresh, washed fruit. Use a scoop to clean the litter box daily. Once a week, empty the box, thoroughly wash and dry it, then refill it with clean litter. Also once a week, wash and dry the bottom of the cage. Thoroughly clean the nest box monthly. Let the rabbit out of the cage every day for exercise and attention from your child and the rest of the family. Most rabbits don't like to be picked up, but they love having someone to play with on the floor, so supervise as your child plays with the rabbit at least a couple of times a day for 20 or 30 minutes each time.

Rabbits are very clean animals and always use one corner of their cage as their toilet. However, when running free in your house, the rabbit may use the floor instead of the litter box. There are ways you can persuade your rabbit to use the litter box instead of the carpet, but some rabbits never learn to use a litter box. Other rabbits can be trained to urinate in one but will leave droppings wherever they go. However, the feces are dry and hard and can be vacuumed up easily. Plastic

Teacher Tip—Rabbits in the Classroom

Rabbits make interesting classroom pets that students can study. When children study a specific animal, they learn more about it and become more sensitive to its needs and behavior. Here are some ways students can study a classroom rabbit.

✔ Students can observe the rabbit and make notes about the animal's physical appearance. They should notice such characteristics as the side-placed eyes, teeth, long ears, short front legs, and long back legs.

✔ Students can watch a rabbit hop and study how the legs move and where they are placed. Let the rabbit run over a smooth area of sand and then study the tracks.

✔ Students can watch the rabbit eating and study how the teeth and lips are used. Does he use his paws? Does he eat quickly or slowly? Does he eat all of his food at once or save some of it?

✔ Students can make different kinds of sounds (nothing too loud or startling, however) from different parts of the classroom and watch how the rabbit listens. Do his ears move together or independently?

✔ Students can give the rabbit different healthy foods to see which he prefers. Which are the rabbit's favorites? What foods does he avoid?

✔ If your classroom rabbit is a baby bunny, students can start a growth chart. They will weigh the rabbit each week and chart his growth—overall length, ear size, and hind-leg lengths. Students can also keep track of the amount of food eaten and compare this to the increases in growth.

Quality rabbit pellets are the foundation of a good diet for your pet.

When he's not molting, a short-haired pet rabbit will need to be brushed about once a week.

Training Your Bunny to Use the Litter Box

Try these tips for litter box-training your bunny:

✔ Prepare the litter box by filling it with your choice of litter and then add a few of the rabbits' droppings so he'll start to understand what the box is for.

✔ When you're ready to let the rabbit run free, take him from his cage and put him in the litter box. Don't force the rabbit to stay there. You don't want him to think he's being punished. He may start digging in the litter and, if you're lucky, get the idea and use the litter box. But if he hops out and uses the carpet instead, don't be discouraged.

✔ If your rabbit uses the carpet or the floor instead of the litter box, merely place the litter box in the spot your rabbit chose.

✔ When the occasional accident does occur, clean the spot with vinegar and water. The vinegar acts as a disinfectant and the smell will deter the rabbit from using that spot in the future.

✔ If your rabbit just never seems to get the hang of using the litter box, give him his free-run time before meals and for a shorter length of time. He'll have less of an urge to go, and with a shorter session outside of his cage, he'll probably wait until he gets back in the cage.

cat boxes work well for rabbits, but the sides should be fairly high because rabbits like to dig in their litter.

Pine and cedar bedding shouldn't be used as litter or bedding because they contain phenol, which causes liver disease. Some cat litters should also be avoided. They contain too much dust, which harms the rabbit's lungs. The best choice for litter is a low-dust cat litter or ground corncob. For bedding, straw is the best choice. Rabbits are very neat and tidy creatures and lick themselves all over, all day. However, even with all this self-grooming, they sometimes need a little bit of help. They require regular brushing (every day or every other day at least) during molting season. When rabbits are not molting, they only require a brushing every week or so, unless you own an Angora whose wool requires special attention. Rabbits also need their toenails clipped because they aren't worn down naturally, as they would be in the wild. Check your pet supply store for brushes and nail clippers appropriate for rabbits.

What to Expect From a Rabbit

Rabbits are very sensitive to changes in their feeding, cleaning, and exercise routines. Changes are stressful and may lead to illness. Symptoms of illness are often subtle changes in appetite, behavior, and/or droppings that even older children will miss, so it is always best to have an adult supervise the care of a rabbit. Children should realize that bunnies feel most secure when they are on the ground, so picking up a bunny and carrying him around is not a good idea. Children can get down to ground level with the bunny to pet and play with him, and they'll have a happier pet.

Rabbit Clubs and Associations

American Checkered Giant Rabbit Club
542 Aspen St. NW
Toledo, OR 97391
(541) 336-2543
E-mail: edwards@fbo.com

American Himalayan Rabbit Association
Rt. 2, Box 232
Pomfret, MD 20675

American Netherland Dwarf Rabbit Club
Rt. 1, Box 51
Mason City, IA 50401
(515) 423-5453

American Rabbit Breeders Association
P.O. Box 426
Bloomington, IL 61702
(309) 664-7500
E-mail: arbapost@aol.com
Web: www.arba.net

California Rabbit Specialty Club
22162 S. Hunter Rd.
Colton, OR 97017

House Rabbit Society
Box 1201
Alameda, CA 94501
(510) 521-4631
E-mail: hrsdp@aol.com
Web: www.rabbit.org

Illinois Rabbit Breeders Association
Box 25
Maquon, IL 61458
(309) 875-3171

Oregon League of Rabbit & Cavy Breeders
26730 SE Currin Rd.
Estacada, OR
97023

Palomino Rabbit Co-Breeders Association
6801 Wooded Acres Rd.
Ocean Springs, MS
39564
(601) 826-3313

Rex Rabbit Club
8780 Fairoaks Rd.
Tracy, CA 95376
(209) 836-3455

Silver Marten Rabbit Club
12365 Ford Hwy.
Clinton, MI
49236
(517) 423-5254

Sugar Gliders

S ugar gliders may look like rodents, but actually they're tiny marsupials—about 12 inches long (including their tail) and weighing only a few ounces. After birth, baby sugar gliders remain in their mother's pouch for about ten weeks. Sugar gliders are native to New Guinea and Australia. Large, movable ears and big black eyes give them expressive faces. Their fur is soft and silky to the touch. They are generally gray in color, with a black stripe running from the nose to the base of the tail. The tail is bushy and also gray except the last one to two inches, which are black. The underside of a sugar glider is white or cream-colored. Along the sides of the body is the gliding membrane, called the patagium. It stretches from the front to the rear legs and allows the sugar glider to "glide" through the air. A sugar glider's tail is somewhat prehensile, and the animal can use it to aid in steering during a glide and for carrying leaves and other bedding material into the nest. Sugar gliders live about 10 to 15 years, so any sugar glider you purchase will be around to grow up with your child.

Purchasing a Healthy Sugar Glider

If you decide to purchase a sugar glider, find out first if it is legal in your state or locality to own one of these animals. The laws and situations are different in every area, and because the exotic animal market is still in its infancy, rules are changing all the time. A recently weaned sugar glider that has received daily handling from about one week out of the pouch is the best choice for a new pet. At this age, a

Sugar gliders may look like rodents, but actually they're tiny marsupials.

well-socialized sugar glider will readily accept a new owner and will easily adjust to a new home. If you are unable to locate a glider younger than ten weeks out of the pouch, select a glider on the basis of friendliness over age. A friendly glider—even if a bit older—will make a better pet than a frightened, unsocialized younger animal. If you can give your sugar glider plenty of attention, he will be quite happy as a single pet. However, if you decide to purchase two gliders, it is best to get them at the same time. If your new pets are already well socialized, it should only take a day or two for them to adjust to their new environment. Getting both gliders at the same

Any simple pine box will make an excellent nest box for your sugar glider.

time prevents either one of them from developing an ownership of the cage, which could cause problems with introducing a companion. Your new pets should be friendly, eat well on their own, have clear eyes, and no nasal discharge.

Housing and Accessories

A single pet can be housed in a cage that is about 20" deep by 20" wide by 24" high. It is best if you can go with an even larger cage because sugar gliders are so active. A medium-sized bird cage (the kind designed for cockatiels) with a wire bottom and a pull-out tray works well and is easy to clean. The cage should be located in an area free from drafts and heating and air-conditioning vents. The temperature of the room or area should be maintained between 70 and 90° F (21 and 32° C). Any doors on the cage should be secured with a J-clip or similar locking device.

Sugar gliders need a nest box or pouch to sleep in during the daytime, and they prefer to nest in high places, so place this toward the top of the cage. A pine bird box approximately 6" x 8" x 6" will work or a plastic container with vent and drain holes will do. Some people use specially made pouches that can be hung in the cage and taken out for traveling with the glider. Suitable bedding material can be made of plain newspaper, paper towels, hay, or non-toxic leaves. If using cloth, avoid loose strings or frayed edges. Gliders may choke on string and have been known to become tangled in thread. The litter in the bottom of the cage should be somewhat absorbent but also easy to clean up. It can be the same material used in the nest box or a commercial product sold in stores. Pine shavings or newspaper work well. Do not use paper with colored inks or cedar shavings.

Gliders also need non-toxic branches (apple, willow, or

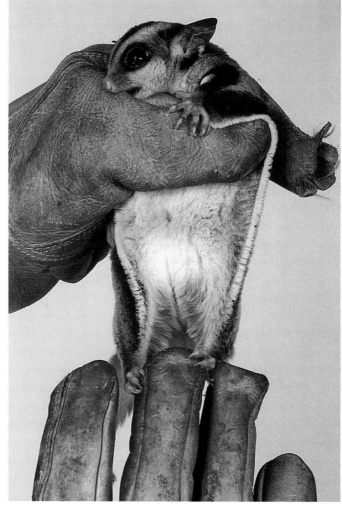

The gliding membrane, called the patagium, stretches from the sugar glider's front to his rear legs, allowing him to glide through the air.

Glider Proofing Your Home

Making your home safe for a dog, cat, or even a rabbit is much different from glider-proofing. Here's how to do it:

✔ Be sure window screens are in good repair and secure so that your glider can't get out.

✔ Be careful with recliners, rockers, and sofa beds. Be certain your sugar glider will not be trapped before you sit down or open a sofa bed. The glider can be crushed or killed by the mechanisms inside.

✔ Make sure toilet lids are down, and always leave the bathroom door closed when the glider is out of his cage. Even with the lid down, gliders can still manage to get inside some toilets.

✔ Be careful of standing water in sinks. Also, close all drains (you wouldn't want your glider ending up in the garbage disposal).

✔ Put a cover on all outlets. Make sure electrical cords behind appliances are not exposed.

✔ Remove anything from a room that you don't want "marked" (including your computer keyboard).

✔ Keep the ceiling fan and all other fans off when sugar gliders are out of their cage.

✔ Put all medications away—you'd be surprised what they can open.

✔ Be sure they can't get into heating or air-conditioning vents.

✔ If you have fish tanks or bowls, make sure they have covers.

✔ Make sure they can't get onto any hot surfaces—the burner on the stove, for example.

✔ Any electric devices, such as portable heaters, should be unplugged.

✔ Make sure fireplaces are completely closed off.

✔ Remove all houseplants—even those that are safe to gliders can be trampled or chewed up.

✔ Cassette tapes should be put away. Sugar gliders will unravel tapes and may even eat them.

✔ Put any extra batteries away. Small animals can gnaw or even swallow small batteries.

aspen) or commercially made parrot perches for climbing and chewing.

Use one or two food dishes for dry items and one dish for moist items, and include a water bottle on the inside of the cage. Because sugar gliders defecate everywhere in their cages, it's best to put food and water on a feeding platform and not on the bottom of the cage under their climbing branches.

Feeding

Sugar gliders should receive 75 percent fruits/vegetables and 25 percent protein in their diet. There are several different commercial sugar glider diets on the market. It is usually best to feed your sugar glider the brand he was used to when you purchased him, provided it was a good, well-rounded diet. But the best way to ensure your pet gets all the nutrients he needs is to provide a variety of foods. Certain foods should be offered daily, while others should be given only occasionally. Some fruits enjoyed by most sugar gliders include watermelon, cantaloupe, grapes, and mangoes. Sugar gliders are also quite fond of apples and oranges. Most gliders are less enthusiastic about peaches, kiwi, strawberries, pears, pineapple, and bananas, and will usually avoid them. It is not surprising that their favorite vegetables tend to be sweet varieties such as corn, sweet potatoes, yams, squash, peas, sweet peppers, and carrots. Do a little experimenting to see what your sugar glider likes. Fruits and vegetables should be fed fresh every evening. Water must be available at all times in a water bottle.

Basic Care

Sugar gliders are nocturnal, making them easier to handle early in the mornings just before they go to sleep or before they normally get up at night. As you handle them daily, they will

Nuts and seeds play an important role in the diet of a pet sugar glider.

become familiar with your scent and will be more trusting. They love to be cuddled. The sugar glider's cage should be cleaned every week. Remove everything thing from the cage and thoroughly wash and dry it, then replace the nesting box and put new litter in the bottom of the cage.

What to Expect From a Sugar Glider

Sugar gliders need plenty of playtime outside of their cages each day. They will explore any opening or secret place they find, so it's best to decide on a specific room of your house that you can glider-proof and use as their playroom.

Because sugar gliders have sharp claws and love to jump and hold onto things like clothing and fingers, they make better pets for older children. However, with careful handling, these animals bond with their owners and become friendly companions.

Web Resource for Sugar Glider Lovers

Try this Web site for more information about sugar gliders:

GliderCentral

http://www.sugarglider.com
Here you'll find a searchable database. Simply type in the name of your state and a list of breeders in your area will come up. You'll also find links to other information about sugar gliders—message boards, articles, where to get supplies for sugar gliders, and vets for sugar gliders (another database, searchable by state).

Index

Age of child 7
Allergies 5
American Academy of Pediatrics 5
Chinchillas 11
—Appearance 11
—Basic care 14
—Clubs 15
—Colors 11
—Dust Baths 14
—Feeding 14
—Housing and accessories 12-13
—Origin 11
—Signs of health 11-12
Classroom pets, choosing 9
Department of Agriculture 7
Department of Natural Resources 7
Department of Wildlife 7
Ferrets 17
—Available colors 17
—Basic care 22
—Behavior 23
—Clubs 21
—Feeding 20-21
—Housing and accessories 19-20
—Legal restrictions 17-18
—Life span 17
—Litter training 19, 22
—Odor 17
—Origin 17
—Selection 18-19
—Web sites 23
Gerbils 25
—Basic care 29
—Color 25
—Feeding 28
—Handling 29
—Housing and accessories 27
—Legal restrictions 26
—Life span 26
—Origin 25
—Selection 25-26
—Size 25
—Social nature 26
Gnawing 8
Guinea pigs 31
—Basic care 34-35
—Breeds 31
—Cavy 31
—Clubs 35
—Feeding 33-34
—Handling 35
—Housing and accessories 32-33
—Life span 31
—Natural habitat 31
—Origin 31
—Selection 32
—Size 31
—Social nature 35
Hamsters 37
—Basic care 40-41
—Cheek pouches 37
—Chinese hamster 37
—Clubs 41
—Feeding 40
—Handling 41
—Housing and accessories 39-40
—Origin 37
—Roborovski's dwarf desert hamster 38
—Russian dwarf hamster 37-38
—Selection 38-39
—Size 37
—Sociability 38
—Syrian hamster 37
Legal restrictions 7
Mice 43
—Available colors 43
—Basic care 46
—Clubs 47
—Feeding 46
—Handling 47
—Housing and accessories 45-46
—Life span 43
—Selection 43, 45
—Size 43
—Social nature 44
Monetary costs 5
Need for company 7
Need for space 5
Rabbits 49
—As classroom pets 55
—Basic care 54
—Breeds 49
—Clubs 57
—Feeding 52
—Handling 55
—Housepets 49
—House Rabbit Society 49
—Housing and accessories 51
—Litter box training 56
—Selection 50
—Signs of illness 51
—Size 49
Rats 43
—Available colors 43
—Basic care 46
—Clubs 47
—Feeding 46
—Handling 47
—Housing and accessories 45-46
—Life span 43
—Rat-proofing your home 47
—Selection 43, 45
—Size 43
Stewart, Martha 11
Sugar gliders 59
—Appearance 59
—Basic care 63
—Feeding 62
—Glider-proofing your home 62
—Handling 63
—Housing and accessories 61
—Legal restrictions 59
—Life span 59
—Origin 59
—Patagium 59
—Selection 59-60
—Size 59
—Sociability 60-61
—Web site 63
Veterinary care 8